Author:
Jacqueline Morley studied English at
Oxford University. She has taught English and
History, and now works as a freelance writer.
She has written historical fiction and non-fiction
for children.

Artist:
David Antram was born in Brighton, England,
in 1958. He studied at Eastbourne College of Art
and then worked in advertising for fifteen years
before becoming a full-time artist. He has
illustrated many children's non-fiction books.

Series Creator:
David Salariya was born in Dundee, Scotland.
He has illustrated a wide range of books and has
created and designed many new series for
publishers both in the UK and overseas. In 1989,
he established The Salariya Book Company. He
lives in Brighton with his wife, illustrator Shirley
Willis, and their son Jonathan.

Editor: **Karen Smith**

Assistant Editor: **Claire Andrews**

Published in Great Britain in 2005 by
Book House, an imprint of
The Salariya Book Company Ltd
25 Marlborough Place, Brighton BN1 1UB

Please visit the Salariya Book Company at:
www.salariya.com

ISBN 0-531-12410-X (Lib. Bdg.)
ISBN 0-531-12390-1 (Pbk.)

Published in 2005 in the United States
by Franklin Watts
An imprint of Scholastic Library Publishing
90 Sherman Turnpike, Danbury, CT 06816

A CIP catalog record for this title is available from
the Library of Congress.

Printed and bound in China.

Manufactured by Leo Paper Products Ltd.

Printed on paper from sustainable forests.

You Wouldn't Want to Be in Alexander the Great's Army!

Join the army and see the world!

Miles You'd Rather Not March

Written by
Jacqueline Morley

Illustrated by
David Antram

Created and designed by
David Salariya

Franklin Watts®
A Division of Scholastic Inc.
NEW YORK • TORONTO • LONDON • AUCKLAND • SYDNEY
MEXICO CITY • NEW DELHI • HONG KONG
DANBURY, CONNECTICUT

Contents

Introduction

I t is the 4th century BC and you are a sheep farmer living in the hilly land just north of Greece known as Macedonia. You Macedonians are tough country people, used to a hard life. Though you might speak Greek and worship Greek gods, the Greeks of the south look down on you as rough and uncivilized foreigners. However, Macedonians have been teaching those soft-living southern Greeks a thing or two recently. Macedonia used to be weak and divided but your previous king, Philip II, made it united and strong and turned the Macedonians into a fighting force that now controls most of Greece. His son, Alexander III, who is only 20, is about to start on a great scheme that his father was planning when he died. He is going to invade the mighty Persian Empire. He needs soldiers, so why not leave those bleak hills, join him and see the world?

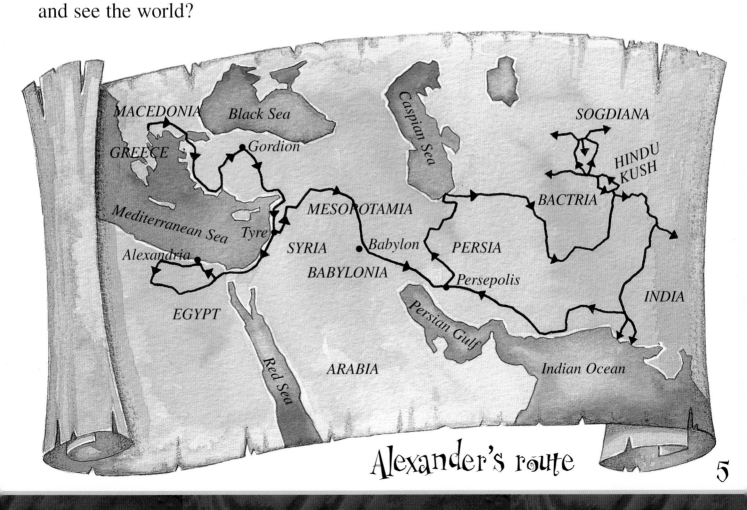

Alexander's route

Joining Up

You like the idea of fighting the Persians, who've been trying for two centuries to conquer Greece. They burned the temples at Athens once, an outrage Alexander has sworn to avenge. You enlist as a foot soldier as you can't afford the sort of horse that is needed in the cavalry. Now you are looking forward to some action. Macedonian infantry is famous for its deadly attack.

There's no need to push – I can't go any faster!

YOU'RE KEEN TO JOIN King Philip's army when you hear what a great life it is. Rich rewards from plunder and never a defeat!

Handy Hint

If people don't listen, burn down their city. Alexander burned Thebes as a lesson to the rest of Greece that they should do what he tells them to do.

Army Training:

INFANTRY DRILL IS TOUGH. You have to act like part of a machine. In tight rows of four men, 16 deep, you practice rushing at the enemy. No stumbling! No hanging back! And keep those pikes lowered evenly — they're over 13 feet (4 m) long!

IN 336 BC KING PHILIP was assassinated by a bodyguard. Alexander's scheming mother, Olympias, may have set this up.

YOUR NEW KING, Alexander, is a born leader and very ambitious. He means to be an even greater conqueror than his father.

ALEXANDER soon shows who's master. When the Greek city of Thebes defies him, he orders the army to sack it and show no mercy.

334 BC: Alexander Sets Off

Alexander is marching into Asia Minor (modern Turkey), to free its Greek city states from Persian rule. It's tough being on the march all day, weighed down with armor, weapons, and a backpack with bedroll. You march about (15 miles) 24 km a day. This is the most that can be managed by the baggage train — the long line of animals and carts carrying tents, medical supplies, tools, and siege engines.

ALEXANDER and his generals ride while the rest of the army marches.

Officer of the cavalry

From Cavalry...

ALEXANDER'S FIGHTING FORCE numbers over 37,000. There are Macedonian and Greek cavalry units, tough Macedonian foot soldiers, Greek hoplites, archers, slingers, and shield bearers.

I wish the folks back home could see me now!

Handy Hint

Be like Alexander — decisive! He undid the famous Gordian knot which no one in four centuries could unravel. He just cut it!

Architect

Foot soldier

...to Poets

AS WELL AS FIGHTING MEN, a host of back-up people are needed, about one for every three soldiers: servants to pitch the tents and cook, grooms for the horses, transport guards, doctors, architects, engineers and surveyors to design bridges and siege equipment, and carpenters and blacksmiths to make them.

ALEXANDER'S PERSONAL TEAM includes bodyguards, secretaries, pages, seers to interpret the will of the gods, philosophers, poets, musicians, and a historian to record his deeds!

Poet

9

ALEXANDER'S CATAPULTS launch deadly bolts against the defenders on the walls of Tyre.

Siege tower

332 BC: Siege of Tyre

Your army has swept through Asia Minor, freeing its Greek cities and making the Persian king Darius and his army flee for their lives. Mission accomplished! You'd like to go home now. But Alexander has other plans. He means to be master of the rest of Darius's vast empire. First he must control the ports of the eastern Mediterranean, so that the Persians cannot launch a sea attack on Greece while he is campaigning further east. Now the fighting gets really nasty. The rich port of Tyre is loyal to Persia. It won't open its gates like the Greek cities. You have to mount a grueling seven-month siege.

TYRE'S DEFENSE. You think it would be great to be first over the walls — until the port's defenders pour down red-hot sand. It is agony when it gets beneath your armor!

Handy Hint

Avoid being chosen as an envoy to Tyre. The last one was thrown into the sea.

TYRE IS CAPTURED, at last, in August 332 BC. To show what happens to people who resist him, Alexander has 2,000 of its men crucified.

TYRE STANDS ON A WALLED ISLAND. To get his siege towers into firing range Alexander builds a huge causeway from the mainland .You're nearly burned alive when the defenders float fireships into it.

11

332-331 BC: In Egypt

Marching south from Tyre, you've reached Egypt, the richest of Persia's subject lands. The Egyptians have welcomed you. They had heard it was dangerous to resist Alexander and they hate the Persians anyway. Your life here is quite enjoyable. There is plenty to eat and lots to see but you think the Egyptians are odd. They worship strange gods with animal faces and believe their king is a god on earth. Now that Alexander is their king some Macedonians think he has begun behaving too much like a god himself. He consulted an oracle at a temple in the desert and was allowed to see the sacred image of its god, Ammon. No one knows what the god told him, but afterward its priest addressed him as the son of Ammon.

ALEXANDER HAS BEEN CROWNED PHARAOH of Egypt, a title that means king. Egyptian civilization is much older than that of Greece.

Handy Hint

When lost, look for a friendly omen. In the desert Alexander followed the flight of two crows.

A NEW CITY. Alexander has found the perfect site for a new Greek city on the Egyptian coast. He will call it Alexandria.

ON HIS TRIP TO THE ORACLE Alexander and his companions got caught in a blinding sandstorm and lost their way.

ALEXANDER AND HIS MEN were desperate with thirst when a downpour saved them. Some tried to catch the rain in their mouths.

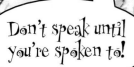

Don't speak until you're spoken to!

331 BC: The Battle of Gaugamela

From Egypt Alexander has marched into Mesopotamia. He is getting close to Persia and King Darius knows there has to be a showdown. He offers Alexander half his empire if he will turn his army back. Alexander refuses and laughs. He meets the Persians in battle near the village of Gaugamela. You are victorious though outnumbered five to one. With a brilliant cavalry charge Alexander reaches Darius's chariot. The Persian king retreats and his forces panic and flee.

Before the Battle

A BAD OMEN — an eclipse of the moon! But Alexander's seer says it is only bad for Darius.

THE PERSIANS have driven stakes into the ground near Gaugamela to cripple your men and horses as they charge.

DARIUS'S ARMY also has fearsome chariots, with wheels set with rotating blades to slice your legs.

14

Handy Hint

Don't let enemies escape to fight again. At Gaugamela you follow and kill them as they flee.

Are we winning?

THE BATTLE raises such clouds of dust that in the end no one can see. You spot fleeing Persians by the sound of their whips lashing their mounts.

15

330 BC: Sacking of Persepolis

Hands off pal – I'm having that!

When you joined the army you reckoned on doing plenty of looting — that is how generals pay their men. But never in your wildest dreams did you imagine the riches of Persepolis. It is the heart of the Persian Empire, housing Darius's stupendous palace and treasury. Alexander has called it the most hateful city in Asia, because its kings have menaced Greece for centuries and once set fire to Athens. He tells you to show no mercy and to help yourself to anything, except the royal treasure — that's for him. Gold, silver, and silks galore are up for grabs and soon your companions are fighting and even killing each other for the richest prizes. Don't hold on to something for too long or your hand may be cut off!

YOU ENTERED PERSIA through a narrow gorge, a death-trap where ambushers rained down boulders that killed many men.

ALEXANDER SITS in triumph on the throne of Darius, who has fled through the mountains to seek help further north.

SOME RICH FAMILIES put on their finest clothes and throw themselves to their death from the city walls, rather than face slaughter.

ALEXANDER STAYS four months in Persepolis. Just before he leaves, its palace is destroyed in a raging fire which he may have lit.

330 BC: King Darius Dies

Alexander marches you until you're ready to drop. In a small, lightly armed force you're rushing ahead of the main army to catch Darius. He spent the winter further north, in Media. He was safe there while all routes were icebound, but now you're after him. After a grueling 450-mile-march (720 km) at top speed, you reach Media to find Darius has fled to get help from the Bactrians, an unruly frontier people. Following him at breakneck speed, 16 hours at a stretch, you reach the Parthian desert, near the Caspian Sea.

Pursuing Darius

DARIUS wanted the retreating Bactrian allies to stop and help him fight. They wouldn't agree and took him prisoner instead.

MEN DROPPED FROM EXHAUSTION and horses were galloped to death as Alexander chased the Bactrians. He traveled 40 miles (65 km) in one night.

Today an officer returns to camp with gruesome news. Wandering in search of water, he came across an abandoned cart. Its dying horses were stuck with spears. Lifting its covering he discovered the bodies of Darius and two servants, stabbed by his treacherous Bactrian allies.

Handy Hint

To win a nation over, show its dead ruler respect. Alexander gives Darius a grand funeral.

Good news for us – bad news for him!

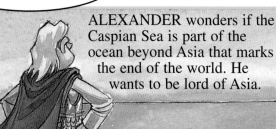

ALEXANDER wonders if the Caspian Sea is part of the ocean beyond Asia that marks the end of the world. He wants to be lord of Asia.

THE ARMY is getting fed up. Darius is no longer a threat, so why can't you all go home? In a rousing speech Alexander scorns such feebleness.

ON INTO BACTRIA. To cross the desert quickly, Alexander orders all carts and excess goods, even his own, to be burned. They slow the army down.

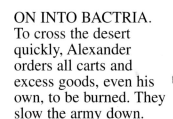

329 BC: Crossing the Hindu Kush

When you left Macedonia, you didn't expect to end up frozen in a snow-blocked pass! That's what has happened to many of your companions, as Alexander leads you through the Hindu Kush mountains to Bactria (modern Uzbekistan). Its rebellious leaders are a threat he can't ignore and before going further east he must destroy them. The journey is terrible. Men and horses are lost in snowdrifts or through exhaustion. You're struggling with snow blindness, frostbite, and painful breathing in the thin air. In narrow places you go single file, which means that the whole army — now 64,000 soldiers, back-up staff, pack animals, and the families of men who've gained wives along the way — will take over a fortnight to thread the pass.

KEEP MOVING. Too weak and tired to go another step? You'll very quickly die of cold if your companions don't rouse you (left).

CROSSING THE RIVER OXUS. There are no trees to build a bridge, so ox-skin tent covers are blown up to form rafts (right).

FIERY TEMPER. Alexander, always hot-headed, is getting worse. He kills his close friend Cleitus in a drunken rage (left).

PERSIAN HABITS. Alexander's officers dislike his new Persian ways. He wants them to kiss their fingers to him in the style of the Persian greeting (right).

327 BC: Scaling the Sogdian Rock

The Bactrians and the neighboring Sogdians are not easy people to subdue. They do not fight proper battles. Instead they swoop in lightning raids, then vanish to their bases in the mountains. One wild Sogdian clan has been defiantly jeering at Alexander from its fortress on the top of a particularly high and craggy peak. Alexander promises to reward any of his men who will climb the sheer rockface by night, using ropes and tent pegs as crampons. Three hundred make the attempt. Thirty fall to their death, but by dawn the rest have reached the summit that overhangs the fortress.

THE SOGDIANS believe they are safe in their fortress. They hurl insults at Alexander's envoy. 'Get yourselves wings' they shout.

Did you say 'Hang on a minute?!'

Handy Hint

If your army is freezing, make a whole forest into bonfires, as Alexander did!

A CLIMBER signals Alexander from the top. Seeing men up there, the Sogdians think it's the whole army and so surrender.

A TERRIBLE ICE STORM causes many deaths. Furious torrents of hail numb men so they collapse and freeze.

FROZEN STIFF. People are found frozen to tree trunks, dead but still upright and as if talking to each other.

23

326 BC: Into India

Alexander has reached India (in an area that is modern-day Pakistan) and still Asia stretches ahead of him, apparently without end. The rulers here are rich, powerful, and well organized. Rajah Porus comes to fight Alexander at the head of a huge army that includes 100 war-trained elephants. In battle they are terrifying. They seize men with their trunks, dash them to the ground, and trample them under their feet. The best defense is to hack at their legs and cripple them. It's a tough fight but, as always, Alexander and his forces manage to win.

Uurrgh!

MONSOON! You're learning an awful lot. You had never heard of a monsoon until now. After 70 days of rain the camp is flooded.

SNAKES, searching for dry spots, get into everything. There are huge cobras in the tents and little, poisonous ones inside the cooking pots.

YOU CAN TRY SLEEPING in a hammock to keep away from snakes, but the creatures can slither down a tree trunk or drop from above.

Handy Hint

Remember that panicked elephants can trample their own soldiers as much as yours!

NEXT, the army is off into the Punjab, across foaming rivers where men and boats are dashed to bits on the rocks. How far does Alexander mean to go?

THE ARMY has had enough and tells Alexander it will not go any further. When his speeches are unable to persuade the soldiers, he sulks in his tent.

KNOWING he will have to give in, Alexander seeks an excuse. Conveniently, his seer says the omens are unlucky so it would be unwise to continue.

25

325 BC: The Gedrosian Desert

The journey home is going terribly wrong. Alexander plans to return you home via the Indian Ocean coast, looking for harbors for a sea route east. This means 60 days spent crossing the Gedrosian Desert. The army can't carry enough food to last the journey, so supplies were to be landed along the coast by ships ordered in India. But monsoon winds have stopped them sailing, so no food has come. You have to go on without food or water.

Who'd have thought it would end like this?

IT'S BETTER TO TRAVEL AT NIGHT. By day the sun is blistering and you sink up to your knees in soft sand that scorches your flesh.

PEOPLE who are too sick or exhausted to walk are left behind. No one has the strength to carry them or give them any help.

Only a quarter of you survive the ordeal of weeks in the baking wilderness. Over 60,000 people perish. That's more than everyone who died in Alexander's battles.

Handy Hint

If you're dying of thirst and reach water, don't drink too much, too fast. It will kill you. Many die this way.

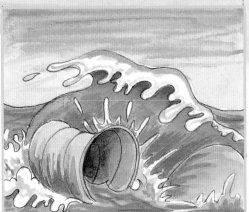

SOON MEN START KILLING THE HORSES (pretending they have died) and, since there is not a scrap of wood to make a fire, they eat them raw.

A STORM in far off hills makes a stream into a flash flood one night, sweeping away the baggage train, its men, women, and children.

323 BC: The Death of Alexander

After eight years away, Alexander has returned in triumph, lord of lands stretching from Greece to the Punjab. He bases his court at Babylon, the winter capital of the Persian kings. After settling there for just a few months, he announces plans to go off to Arabia on a new campaign. And North Africa is still to be conquered! But none of this will happen now. He is taken ill suddenly with a violent fever and is at the point of death.

Before He Died

BIG WEDDING. Alexander is keen for Greeks and Persians to mix well in his empire. In a mass ceremony he and 90 Macedonian officers wed Persian brides.

OLD SOLDIERS like you become unhappy and feel unwanted in an army full of Persian recruits. Alexander had to put an end to their angry protest.

We'll never see another like him.

BABYLONIAN seers warn Alexander not to enter Babylon on his way west, so he goes around it to come in the opposite way.

28

You say farewell to your great leader, filing past him one by one. Speechless, he raises a hand in greeting. The very next day the conqueror of one of the largest empires ever known is dead, at age 32.

Handy Hint

If you believe in omens, and seers warn you not to do something, perhaps you'd better not.

WHAT NEXT? Alexander's generals are soon fighting over how to share his empire. Whose army should you join? Or perhaps you have had enough of war by now.

Glossary

Ammon A Libyan god honored by the Egyptians as a form of their own creator-god, Amun.

Bolt A short, all-metal arrow that was shot from a catapult.

Catapult A large piece of machinery with a wooden framework that fired bolts and large stones.

Causeway A roadway built on an artificial mound.

Cavalry The regiments of an army that fight on horseback.

Cobra A poisonous Indian snake that puffs out its head and neck when angry.

Crampons Metal spikes used to give climbers a foothold on sheer rock.

Envoy An official sent by one leader to another, to deliver a message or discuss a matter.

Fireships Ships deliberately set on fireand floated against the enemy's defenses to burn them.

Hoplite A heavily armed foot-soldier with a large round shield.

Infantry The portion of an army that fights on foot.

Monsoon A wind that brings long periods of torrential rain to southern Asia in summer.

Omen An object or event that is supposed to foretell some future good or evil.

Oracle A person through whom a god is said to speak.

Punjab A region of the Indian subcontinent in what is now Pakistan. Its name, meaning 'five rivers', refers to the five tributaries of the River Indus that flow through it, which Alexander's forces had much trouble crossing.

Sandstorm Sand hurled through the air by strong winds.

Seer A professional interpreter of omens.

Shield bearers Lightly armed, fast-moving foot soldiers.

Siege engine A large construction of wood and metal designed to launch missiles against, or over, defensive walls.

Silphium Probably the plant *asafoetida*, which is used in herbal medicine.

Stronghold A fortified place capable of resisting attack.

Index